This book is dedicated to my mom, Renee,
who always celebrates holidays in a big way!
There was always room at our table for anyone who
was alone during the holidays. Good food, family,
friends and laughter bring all of us together,
and are the best parts of the holidays.
My mom was also so great about decorating
our home from top to bottom for every holiday
making them all equally special.

EFFIE'S FRIENDSGIVING

Author : Jennifer Morhaime   Illustrator : Hameoart

J. Morhaime Books Publication
Hardback ISBN: 979-8-9852890-3-9

Effie's
Friendsgiving

BY JENNIFER MORHAIME
ILLUSTRATED BY HAMEOART

Effie spent all weekend making invitations for all her friends.
"Mom, I want everyone to be able to celebrate!
My friends all have such different backgrounds from ours;
I cannot wait to all come together and share."
Effie sighs as she crawls into bed.
"Effie, I am so proud of you for coming up with this party."
Mom kisses Effie and says "Good Night my sweet little girl."

You are invited to

EFFIE'S FRIENDSGIVING!

• • •

Sunday
December 4th

12:00 PM

Effie's House

Bring your favorite Holiday
Treat to Share.

The next day, Effie immediately passes invitations
to all her friends on the bus heading to school.
"This is so great Effie! My family celebrates Hanukkah,
and I can't wait to teach you all how to play dreidel."
Billy claps excitedly.
"Jessie, you don't celebrate Christmas either right?" George asks.
Jessie responds shyly, "No, we celebrate Diwali. I love all the bright
colors and shapes. It reminds me of painting, which you know I love!"

When they arrive at school, Effie hands out the rest of the invitations to the class.

"Good morning class, today we have a new student joining us. Please welcome Flynn," Mrs. Smith calls.

"Flynn, why don't you find a seat and we'll get started for the day."

As the class heads out to recess, Effie pulls an invitation out of her bag and hands it to Flynn. "Hi Flynn. I'm having a little holiday get together and I'd love if you could join us."

Flynn smiles and thanks Effie as they head out the door.

As the class comes back in, Mrs. Smith tells them to take their seats quickly because they have a special guest, Mr. Ridley the Librarian.

"Class, as you know, there are many holidays in the Fall and Winter season. Today we're going to look at some books about how everyone celebrates." Mr. Ridley pulls a few books off his cart as he continues. "By show of hands, how many of you have heard of Christmas? Hanukkah? Great, who here celebrates something other than these two?"

Violet, Kiki and Sammy all raise their hands ready to share.
Mr. Ridley starts, "Violet, would you like to share what
your family celebrates?"
"Um, we celebrate the Solstice, so we have Yule
instead of Christmas." Violet shares.
"Thank you, Violet. Sammy what does your family celebrate?"
Mr. Ridley asks.

"We celebrate the Lunar New Year. This year it is the Rabbit just like me! We'll be celebrating in a BIG way!" Sammy Cheers. "Wonderful Sammy. We've got a book all about the Lunar New Year in this cart and it explains all about the zodiac signs too. Kiki, you're next please." Mr. Ridley directs. Just then, the bell rings, so Mr. Ridley lets the kids pick books from the cart, as they head out to the buses.

When Effie gets home, she tells her mom all
about her day, and the new classmate, Flynn.
The next morning the ground is covered in snow.
"Oh mom, I hope this doesn't ruin my party plans."
"Effie don't stress about the snow, it should be gone
in time for your party. Now get ready for school or
you'll miss the bus." Effie's mom instructs.'

As the day went on, the snow melted and Effie was feeling better about her upcoming party. She even jumped in the puddles and sang to herself all the way up the driveway.

"Mom, can Jessie come over and help me decorate for the party?" Effie asked. "Sure. Why don't you invite Evan and Jessie for dinner and we can help you?" Effie's mom replied.

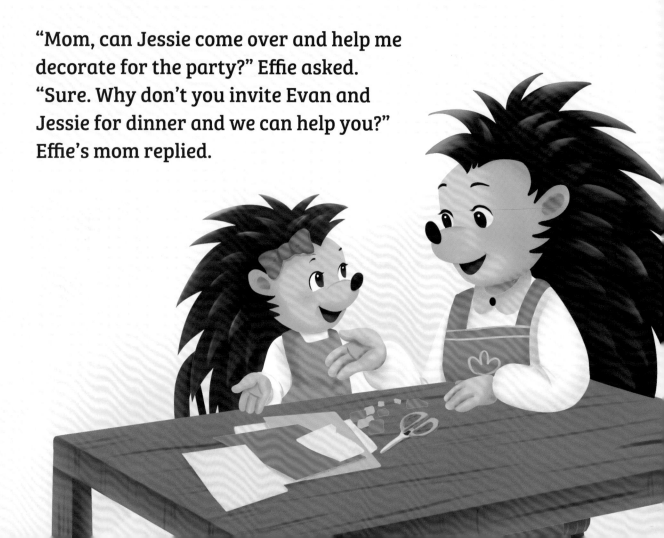

Effie calls Jessie and invites her and her dad over for dinner.
Effie and Jessie start turning the family room into a colorful
display of paper rings, lights, and tissue paper flowers.
They cut fall leaves and pumpkins, candy canes and
snowflakes out and line the center
of the table.

Evan turns to Hannah and says with a chuckle,
"Hannah, can you tell which holiday they are celebrating?
Is it Fall? Winter? Or Spring?"

"I know, right! Effie wants to make sure all her friends feel celebrated. She has been so busy trying to make this as unique as she is. Would you like to join us for the party and help me supervise?" Hannah responds. "I'd love to. Thanks. You are so nice to be hosting this."

The next few days were filled with school, cooking and more decorating. Sunday finally arrives and it is the day of the party. Effie wakes up and runs downstairs to start cooking with her mom. "It's party day! It's party day!" Effie shouts with excitement. "The turkey is dressed and is ready for the oven. Can you grab the door Effie?" Effie's mom asks carrying the large roasting pan with the turkey inside.

Effie runs to the family room and starts setting up her sugar cookie decorating station – her favorite part of the holidays – creating delicious masterpieces of frosting and candy.

The table is set with plates in all shapes and colors. Effie puts her gingerbread house she made at school in the center of the table too. The room is ready for the celebration!

Jessie and Evan arrived early to help with the final setup and cooking.
Billy arrived early too with a tray full of golden potato latkes and applesauce, and a bag with a big dreidel painted on it.
He immediately puts out little bags of gold coins at each plate.
"These are for when we play dreidel." he tells the girls
with a smile.

George, Violet and Kiki all showed up next. Kiki has a tray of cookies, Violet has some beverages, and a yule log cake and George has sides for the feast - mashed potatoes, and roasted veggies.
Sammy and Charlie get dropped off right behind them with arms full of food. "What is all this?" Effie asks.

"My mom made her homemade crispy spring rolls and pot stickers, and Charlie has long noodle salad and sesame balls." Sammy has a giftbag too. After dropping off her food she starts putting little red envelopes on each plate next to the chocolate coins Billy brought. "These are for luck!" She smiles again.

The table is filling up and the kids are all laughing and playing. Some are decorating cookies and Billy is trying to teach a few how to play dreidel.

The doorbell rings and Hannah answers.
"Hello, welcome to Effie's Friendsgiving."
"Hi, I'm Flynn. I just moved to town and Effie invited me.
I brought some Jelly donuts and Popcorn." Flynn says.
"Welcome Flynn. The kids are all in the other room. Go enjoy."
As Hannah was about to close the door, she sees
the neighbors coming down the path.

"Hi Talivia! Did you bring your Kinara to share?" Hannah greets.
"Hi Mrs. Hedgehog. Yes, I've got all the candles ready to light
if you'll help me. This is my new sister Anna Capri. I hope
it's ok for her to join." Talivia smiles.
"Of course! Your mom told me you were adding a new member
to the family soon. Effie wants everyone to feel welcome
at her party, so please come in and join the festivities."
Anna Capri and Talivia slowly join the other kids.

"Thank you all so much for coming to my first Friendsgiving. I'm hoping we can go around the table and share about our holidays and family traditions. My mom made us a turkey and I made my favorite fall treat - Pumpkin Bars. I also love decorating cookies for Christmas, so I wanted to share that tradition with you all too." Effie gleams.

"Thank you for inviting me, Effie. My family celebrates Hanukkah and Christmas, so I brought a menorah to light candles. We light the candles for 8 nights to represent the miracle of the Maccabees oil that lasted eight days instead of one. On Christmas eve, we watch movies and string popcorn garland for our tree, although we eat more than we string."
Flynn winks.

"Along with the Lunar New Year feast, we gave each of you a lucky red envelope called hangbao, which represents good wishes and luck for the new year."
Sammy claps while Charlie smiles.

"Hi everyone, I'm Talivia
I live next door. My family
celebrates Kwanzaa.
I brought my Kinara and
the 7 Candles to light.

Each candle represents one of the 7 pillars of Kwanzaa, and the colors represent struggle, hope and people of African descent.
I also brought some roasted Sweet Potato Casserole – my favorite part is the marshmallows. This is my new foster sister Anna Capri, she just joined our family this week."
"I brought some peppermint bark to share."
Anna adds with a smile.

"My family celebrates the solstice this time of year, so we sip on warm cozy drinks, sit around the fire and we write down our wishes for the new year on paper and then tear them up and burn them in hopes they will come true." Violet chimes.

"My family celebrates Ramadan which is a month-long holiday that ends with Eid. It changes time of year as it rotates on a Lunar calendar, so we just make our Date Cookies for holiday parties this time of year so we can join. Jessie, you're next." Kiki passes.

"My family celebrates Diwali. We decorate the home with lanterns and lots of color. It is magical. We celebrate the victory of light over darkness. My dad made some Laddu for dessert. And I made some Jalebi because they are my favorite."
Jessie slumps into her chair shyly.

"My family also celebrates Hanukkah! I gave you each a bag of gelt, which are chocolate coins, and we'll use them when we play the dreidel game."   Billy shares next.

"Thank you everyone – Let's eat!" Effie chimes.
After eating Billy and Flynn light the Menorah and Talivia lights her Kinara with Hannah's help. Some of the kids return to their dreidel game while others finish their cookie decorating.

"Look everyone, it started snowing again! Let's go play!"
George jumps up with glee.

Everyone gets up from the table and puts on their coats and hats and head outside for an afternoon of snowball fights, sledding and snowman building!

Latke Recipe

Latkes are shredded potato pancakes, fried, and served with applesauce and sometimes sour cream during Hanukkah. They are fried in oil to remember the miracle of the oil lasting 8 days!

2 pounds of shredded potato
(you can use thawed frozen hashbrown shreds)
1 parsnip shredded
1 medium yellow onion
2-3 eggs
1 Tablespoon Onion Powder
1 Tablespoon Garlic Powder
Salt and pepper to taste
Canola Oil for frying

Add oil to a sauté pan about 1" high.
Grate potatoes, parsnip, and onion. Squeeze out as much liquid as you can from the shredded mix. Warm the oil on medium heat. Add 2 eggs and spices and whisk together. Add drained potato mix to the eggs and mix. Test the batter by trying to clump together the mix. If it falls apart add an additional egg. If it clumps together, you're ready to fry.
Test the temperature of the oil by dropping 1 piece of the shredded potato into it. If it sizzles, then the oil is ready. Drop 3-4 scoops into the pan and fry on each side until golden brown. Prep a cookie sheet with paper towels on the bottom as latkes come out of the oil you can drain them on the sheet. Some like to also add a little salt on top while hot.

Grandma Renee's Pumpkin Bars

4 eggs   1 cup oil
2 cups pumpkin pie filling
(need the big can of Libby's, but won't use it all)
1 2/3 cups sugar

2 cups flour
2 tsp. baking powder
2 tsp. cinnamon
1 tsp. salt
1 tsp. baking soda

Beat eggs, pumpkin, sugar and oil until fluffy. Add dry ingredients. Spread batter evenly in ungreased 9x13 Jelly Roll Pan. Bake at 350 for 25-30 minutes. Cool and frost with cream cheese frosting. Yield: 3-4 dozen

Victoria's Date Cookies

Dough
3 cups flour
1 cup unsalted butter
1 Tablespoon ground cardamom
1 Tablespoon yeast
1/2 teaspoon baking powder
1/3 teaspoon cinnamon
1 cup Warm water
let the dough set for an hour

Date Filling
2 cups Brown Dates – remove seed
1 teaspoon cardamom

Preheat oven to 350.
Pour the yeast and water into the bowl and let sit for about 10 minutes or until it starts to foam. Melt the butter until soft but not hot. Add the dry ingredients and butter to the yeast water. Once combined, cover and let rest for 1 hour. While the dough rests, make the date filling. Mash dates in a sauce pan on low heat, then slowly add a teaspoon of cardamom until it becomes a soft and smooth mash. Do not overheat. Using a rolling pin, roll the dough flat and thin, you may want to roll in 2 batches. Spread out the mashed date paste to the edge of the dough and roll tightly from the long side. Slice by using a knife and place pinwheel cookies on a parchment lined cookie sheet; repeat until all the dough and paste have been used. Brush the cookies with a mix of egg and some vanilla for a beautiful color and bake till bottom is brown and top is an even golden brown.

*Recipe shared by Effie's friend Victoria Abdulrahman and Family!

Cream Cheese Frosting
3-oz package cream cheese
½ cup butter

1 tsp vanilla
2 cups powdered sugar

Soften cream cheese and butter. Beat until creamy. Add vanilla. Gradually add powdered sugar until smooth.

*Recipe shared by Renee Levy "Effie's Grandma." We love you "Maya!"

Lunar Dumplings (Potstickers)

Dumplings are one of the 7 Lucky Foods to eat
during the Lunar New Year. They represent wealth.

Filling
1 lb ground chicken or pork
3 cloves of garlic minced
1/4 cup green onion chopped
2 cups finely chopped cabbage
1/3 cup fresh ginger minced
1/2 teaspoon red pepper flakes
1 Tablespoon soy sauce
1 teaspoon white wine vinegar
Package of wonton wrappers

Mix all ingredients in a large bowl. Place a spoonful of filling in the middle of each wrapper. Wet the edge with water and seal the pockets. Use the tines of a fork to crimp the edge to make sure it is sealed. Preheat a skillet with a little oil, fry the bottoms of the dumplings until they are golden on the bottom, you may need to do this in batches. Once the bottoms are browned, carefully add 2 Tablespoons of water to the pan, cover the dumplings and let them steam cook for 3-5 minutes. Clean out the pan between batches so that there is no water in the pan when frying.

Cookies and Cream Peppermint Bark

2 cups of chocolate chips (semi sweet or dark)
2 cups of White Chocolate chips
1 1/2 teaspoons peppermint extract
6 Oreo cookies crushed
3 candy canes crushed
Red and Green Sprinkles

Prepare a cookie sheet with foil - shiny side up and spray with nonstick cooking spray. Place Oreos in a Ziplock bag and crush them with a spoon or rolling pin. Set aside and crush candy canes the same way.

Place the semisweet or dark chocolate chips in a microwave safe bowl. Place in the microwave and warm in 20 second intervals until chocolate is melted. Once melted, stir in 3/4 teaspoon of the peppermint extract. Pour onto cookie sheet and spread evenly. Let cool while you repeat the process with the white chocolate chips. Spread out the white chocolate sprinkle the crushed Oreos and candy canes all over the chocolate. Then add red and green sprinkles for flare. Let cool completely, then break up the bark and place into an airtight container.

Jessie's Jalebi

1 cup all-purpose flour
2 Tablespoons corn flour
1/8 teaspoon Turmeric
1/2 cup plain yogurt

1/2 cup water (more if needed)
1/2 teaspoon baking soda
1 teaspoon lemon juice
Oil or Ghee for frying

Sugar Syrup
1 cup sugar
1/2 to 3/4 cup water
1 pinch of saffron (optional)
1/4 teaspoon cardamom
1 tsp Lemon juice

Mix the flour, corn flour, turmeric and baking soda in a large bowl. Once combined, add yogurt, water and lemon juice. Batter should be soft and smooth, add 1 tablespoon of water at a time. For best results let batter ferment on the counter for 10 hours. Heat oil in a deep pan. Transfer the fermented batter into a piping bag or Ziplock (cut the corner off). While the oil is heating, in a small saucepan combine sugar and 1/2 cup of water and bring to a boil to let sugar dissolve and thicken. Once you can lift the spoon and see a single sugar string add saffron, lemon juice and cardamom and remove from heat. Add additional water 1 teaspoon at a time so that it does not get too thick. Set aside while you fry the batter. Drop batter into the hot oil in circular spirals. Fry on each side until crisp and golden. Soak the jalebi evenly in the sugar syrup for about 3 minutes and enjoy!

ABOUT THE AUTHOR

Jennifer has been writing short stories and poetry since she was a little girl. Her passion for cooking and entertaining came when she was in college. Effie's Friendsgiving is a collaboration of her two passions, writing and cooking. Effie's Adventures is Jennifer's dream come true and cannot wait to see Effie grow. Jennifer lives in Renton, Washington with her loving and supportive husband and two beautiful boys.

www.effiesbooks.com   🅾 effies_books   f effiesbooks

ABOUT THE ILLUSTRATOR

Hameo is a mother and children's book illustrator who puts her heart into all of her art. Her character drawings convey emotions and her choice of color captures the fairy like world of dreams.

www.hameoart.com   🅾 hameoart
em: hameoartstudio@gmail.com

ABOUT THE DESIGNER

Helen is a designer and illustrator, who loves storytelling. Based in the UK, Helen enjoys collaborating with other authors, using her creativity to bring their ideas to life, whilst also producing her own books.

www.helenbarriosbooks.com
🅾 helenbarrios.books   helenbarriosbooks